IN THE SPOTLIGHT

BLACKPINK

K-POP SENSATIONS

Rachel Rose

Lerner Publications ◆ Minneapolis

Lerner Publications Company
An imprint of Lerner Publishing Group, Inc.
241 First Avenue North
Minneapolis, MN 55401 USA

For reading levels and more information, look up this title at www.lernerbooks.com.

Main body text set in ITC Franklin Gothic Std.
Typeface provided by Adobe Systems.

Editor: Annie Zheng **Photo Editor:** Angel Kidd

Library of Congress Cataloging-in-Publication Data

Names: Rose, Rachel, 1968– author.
Title: Blackpink : K-pop sensations / Rachel Rose.
Description: Minneapolis : Lerner Publications, 2025. | Series: In the spotlight (UpDog books) | Includes bibliographical references and index. | Audience: Ages 8–11 | Audience: Grades 4–6 | Summary: "BLACKPINK is one of the biggest girl groups in the world. They are fashion icons, role models, and amazing solo artists. But together, they are unstoppable. Learn more about BLACKPINK!"—Provided by publisher.
Identifiers: LCCN 2024039736 (print) | LCCN 2024039737 (ebook) | ISBN 9798765669181 (library binding) | ISBN 9798765684498 (paperback) | ISBN 9798765679098 (epub)
Subjects: LCSH: Blackpink (Musical group)—Juvenile literature. | Women singers—Korea (South)—Biography—Juvenile literature. | Singers—Korea (South)—Biography—Juvenile literature. | Girl groups (Musical groups)—Korea (South)—Juvenile literature.
Classification: LCC ML3930.B579 R67 2025 (print) | LCC ML3930.B579 (ebook) | DDC 782.4216/3095195 [B]—dc23/eng/20240828

LC record available at https://lccn.loc.gov/2024039736
LC ebook record available at https://lccn.loc.gov/2024039737

Manufactured in the United States of America
1-1011538-53889-10/17/2024

TABLE OF CONTENTS

In Training

The crowd went wild as BLACKPINK sang at Coachella in 2023. It is one of the biggest music events in the world.

The group's name comes from being powerful (black) and pretty (pink).

There are four members.

They are Jennie, Lisa, Jisoo, and Rosé.

Jennie

Lisa

Jisoo

Rosé

They were all trainees at YG Entertainment, a top South Korean record label.

They took singing, rapping, and dancing lessons. They worked very hard.

UP NEXT!

Hitting the stage.

Instant Success

BLACKPINK's first album came out in August 2016.

Their songs “Boombayah” and “Whistle” topped the South Korean music charts.

The group quickly came out with more music.

Soon their songs were hits around the world.

They sing about how to
be both strong and soft.

Many of their songs have both English and Korean lyrics.

STAR STATS

Full name: BLACKPINK

Debut date: August 8, 2016

Home country: South Korea

HONORS:

"Boombayah" was the first and only K-pop debut song to reach one billion views on YouTube.

In 2020, they were the first K-pop girl group to win an award at the MTV Video Music Awards.

In 2023, they became the first K-pop group to headline Coachella.

BLACKPINK has millions of fans. They are called Blinks.

This is a blend of the words "black" and "pink."

Lisa

UP NEXT!

Many talents.

Global Stars

The group has gone on world tours. They've sold out huge stadiums.

They have songs with other big stars such as Selena Gomez and Lady Gaga.

They are not only talented singers.
They are fashion icons too.

They have partnered with famous fashion companies such as Chanel and Christian Dior.

Rosé

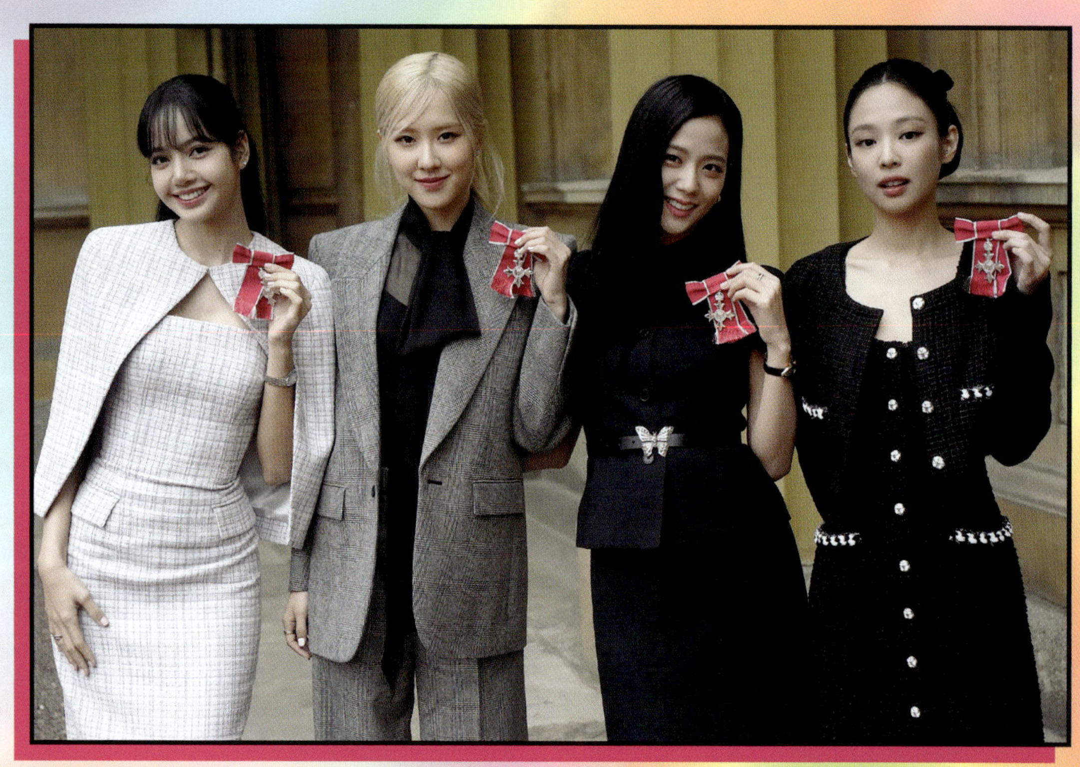

They use their fame to raise awareness about important causes such as climate change.

They donate to many charities.

The members also have solo singing careers.

But they are still together as a group.

BLACKPINK has plenty more to share with the world.

Just like BLACKPINK

BLACKPINK values things that seem as if they are opposite, such as strength and softness. What are things you value that might be at odds? How do they make you stronger?

GLOSSARY

cause: something supported or deserving support

debut: first public appearance

headline: to be the leading performer in a show or event

icon: a person who is admired in a particular field

trainee: someone who trains to become a K-pop idol in South Korea

CHECK IT OUT!

Becker, Trudy. *K-Pop*. Mendota Heights, MN: Focus Readers, 2025.

BLACKPINK Official Website
https://www.blackpinkmusic.com

Kiddle: BLACKPINK Facts for Kids
https://kids.kiddle.co/Blackpink

National Geographic Kids: South Korea
https://kids.nationalgeographic.com/geography/countries/article/south-korea

Schwartz, Heather E. *BTS: K-Pop Fan Favorites*. Minneapolis: Lerner Publications, 2023.

Wood, John. *A Visit to South Korea*. Minneapolis: Bearport, 2023.

INDEX

PHOTO ACKNOWLEDGMENTS

Image credits: Emma McIntyre/Getty Images, pp. 4, 27; AP Photo/Evan Agostini/Invision, p. 5; The Chosunilbo JNS/Getty Images, pp. 6–7, 10, 28; yllyso/Shutterstock, p. 8; Visual China Group/Getty Images, pp. 9, 12, 14; Imaginechina/Alamy, p. 11; THE FACT/Getty Images, p. 13; Chung Sung-Jun/Getty Images, p. 15; Frazer Harrison/Getty Images, p. 16; glamourstock/Alamy, p. 18; ANTHONY WALLACE/Getty Images, p. 19; Christopher Polk/Getty Images, p. 20; Rich Fury/Getty Images, pp. 21, 26; Jeremy Moeller/Getty Images, p. 22; MICHAEL TRAN/Getty Images, p. 23; VICTORIA JONES/Getty Images, p. 24; YUI MOK/Getty Images, p. 25. Design elements: oxygen/Getty Images; Medesulda/Getty Images.

Cover image: Frazer Harrison/Getty Images.